Sports Illustrated

Greatest Pictures

Memorable Images from Sports History

Sports Illustrated

Greatest Pictures

Memorable Images from Sports History

Copyright 1998
Time Inc. Home Entertainment

ISBN 1-883013-56-9
Manufactured in the United States of America
First printing 1998

Library of Congress Catalog Card Number: 98-88560

Sports Illustrated Director of Development: STANLEY WEIL

GREATEST PICTURES
Project Director: MORIN BISHOP
  Senior Editors: JOHN BOLSTER, EVE PETERSON, ANTHONY ZUMPANO
  Associate Editor: THERESA DEAL
  Reporters: WARD CALHOUN, RACHAEL NEVINS
  Photography Editors: BILL BROYLES, JOHN S. BLACKMAR
Designers: BARBARA CHILENSKAS, JIA BAEK

GREATEST PICTURES was prepared by
Bishop Books, Inc.
611 Broadway
New York, New York 10012

Cover photograph:
FERNANDO MEDINA/NBA PHOTOS

TIME INC. HOME ENTERTAINMENT
President: David Gitow
Director, Continuities and Single Sales: David Arfine
Director, Continuities and Retention: Michael Barrett
Director, New Products: Alicia Longobardo
Group Product Managers: Robert Fox, Jennifer McLyman
Product Managers: Christopher Berzolla, Roberta Harris, Stacy
  Hirschberg, Kenneth Maehlum, Daniel Melore
Manager, Retail and New Markets: Thomas Mifsud
Associate Product Managers: Carlos Jimenez, Daria Raehse, Niki
  Viswanathan, Betty Su, Lauren Zaslansky, Cheryl Zukowski
Assistant Product Managers: Jennifer Dowell, Meredith Shelley
Editorial Operations Director: John Calvano
Book Production Manager: Jessica McGrath
Assistant Book Production Manager: Joseph Napolitano
Fulfillment Director: Michelle Gudema
Assistant Fulfillment Manager: Richard Perez
Financial Director: Tricia Griffin
Financial Manager: Amy Maselli
Assistant Financial Manager: Steven Sandonato
Marketing Assistant: Ann Gillespie
  Special thanks to Anna Yelenskaya

We welcome your comments and suggestions about
SPORTS ILLUSTRATED Books. Please write to us at:
SI Books
Attention: Book Editors
PO Box 11016
Des Moines, IA 50336-1016

If you would like to order any of our Hard Cover Collector Edition
books, please call us at 1-800-327-6388. (Monday through Friday,
7:00 a.m.– 8:00 p.m. or Saturday, 7:00 a.m.– 6:00 p.m. Central Time).

10   9   8   7   6   5   4   3   2   1

Contents

Since a picture truly *is* worth a thousand words, we'll be brief in our introduction and cede the stage as quickly as possible to the stirring images collected here. But bear in mind as you enjoy these photographs that *Greatest Pictures* is a history of sports photography, rather than of sports, so not every athletic milestone is represented in these pages. The images come from all across the sporting landscape and from almost every era, and as such represent an impressive sweep of the history of sports. But we make no claim to comprehensiveness. Sure, if all else was equal between two photographs, we chose the one with greater historical significance. But you won't find all of your cherished sports memories here. And though we've included excerpts from *Sports Illustrated* covering selected events and provided some updates of several others, you won't find a lot of trenchant analysis, either. What you will find is a collection of stunning visual scope and aesthetic power. Rather than a timeline of sports history, we've created a one-of-a-kind kaleidoscope of sporting images. Rotate the lens and Babe Ruth, slyly smiling, comes into black-and-white focus; turn it again and there's poor Scott Norwood, in full color but still wide right. Where else will you find basketball legend Larry Bird, whose Celtics teams won three NBA titles in the '80s, following pioneering baseball star Honus Wagner of the Pittsburgh Pirates, who played in the very first World Series?

From Jim Thorpe in his Canton Bulldogs uniform, to Muhammad Ali in exultant rage over the fallen Sonny Liston—one of sport's most famous photographs, and an occasion in which the quality of an image and its historical significance dovetail perfectly—*Greatest Pictures* offers a unique perspective on sports in the twentieth century. The visual emphasis of the volume gives it more range than Omar Vizquel. After all, an eye-catching, stirring photograph can occur in any sport, at any time.

Where else will you find an image like Lou Gehrig's poignant 1939 farewell at Yankee Stadium (opposite) juxtaposed with an in-your-face photograph of Wilt Chamberlain storming the hoop (above)?

Flashing cameras attended every swing during McGwire's quest to break Maris's single-season home run record in 1998.

Additionally, the broad sweep of *Greatest Pictures* provides an occasion, as we approach a new century, for contemplating how much sport has changed over the course of this one. When Wilt Chamberlain scored 100 points against the Knicks in 1962, there were no TV cameras, and few of any kind, present to capture the historic event, which you'll notice is absent from this collection. The reason? There's no good shot of it. The same goes for Roger Maris and his pursuit of Babe Ruth's single-season home run record. The intense media scrutiny Maris faced that season was a harbinger of the future in sports, but still, on the day Maris belted the record breaker, the lighting and the limitations of that era's cameras prevented a quality photograph from being created to record the moment. Can you imagine that happening in this era, when Busch Stadium sparkled like a strobe light from all the flashbulbs each time Mark McGwire took a swing at history in 1998? Not likely. For better and for worse, sport has center stage in our culture and not a second goes undocumented. Paradoxically, as we've moved closer, the athletes have withdrawn in many ways. Take the picture of Ruth, surrounded by adoring kids, on page 150. Would today's sluggers—say, Albert Belle or Barry Bonds—pose for such a photo?

Which is not to say we can't understand the desire of current athletes to protect their privacy. The glare of the spotlight has never been more blinding. Even the genial McGwire, under the microscope all summer long in 1998, showed signs of impatience with the media machine. But the beast, it seems, has an insatiable appetite. We can get scores, highlights and updates, any time, anywhere. We have reverse-angle, super slo-mo replays; we have catcher-cam and pitch charts and FOX Trax. Yet for all of the coverage, for all of the supercharged technology attending sports today, often it is left to the simple, almost quaint, photograph to distill the essence of a moment in sports.

Six-time MVP and 19-time All-Star Kareem Abdul-Jabbar finally walked away from basketball in 1989 after 20 seasons and six NBA titles; he left the game as the career leader in points scored and games played.

Griffith-Joyner dominated the 1988 Olympic Games, cruising to gold medals in the 100- and 200-meter dashes as well as the 4 x 100-meter relay.

Memorable Moments

Some enduring moments in sport are made strictly by the photographer, who snaps his camera at just the right time from the perfect angle to capture an event in a way we may not have noticed with the naked eye. Richard Mackson's picture of the Twins' Dan Gladden touching home plate after colliding with Atlanta catcher Greg Olson in the 1991 World Series is one of these. While Olson performs an involuntary headstand, Gladden's helmet, on the left, seems to levitate. Only a camera shutter could have preserved this instant.

Other moments are dictated by the action: An athlete seizes control at a critical time, or makes the perfect pass, or sinks the winnning bucket at the buzzer, and the camera catches the play. The memorable photo of Bart Starr burrowing in for the winning score in the fabled "Ice Bowl" NFL title game between Dallas and Green Bay in 1967 fits this category.

Still others blend these conditions beautifully. Walter Iooss Jr.'s shot of John Havlicek's famous steal against Philadelphia in the 1965 Eastern Conference finals— every sports fan knows the play, and Celtic broadcaster Johnny Most's legendary call, "Havlicek stole the ball! Havlicek stole the ball!"—is an example of this last. Here was a moment that sealed the 76ers' fate and sent the Celtics into the NBA finals for the seventh year in a row; here was John Havlicek quite literally reaching out and snatching victory for his team. The moment itself was dramatic, and the photograph is equal to the drama, presenting the swoop of Havlicek's arm as he plucks the ball and the expressions of the other players on the court, frozen in the moment their divergent fates are decided.

Instant replay couldn't have given us this; being there in person could scarcely have matched the impact of this visceral still life.

Everything is there in the Havlicek photo, but while a picture freezes a single vista for all time, it is by no means a static entity. Hindsight can ascribe deeper meaning to the tableau. Take the shot of Florence Griffith Joyner on the opposite page. This image of triumph now imparts a bittersweet twinge in light of the record-breaking sprinter's tragic death at 38 in 1998.

The picture of Dwight Clark's famous catch in the 1981 NFC title game on page 14 is another example of a moment's malleability. Since the shot was taken from such a low angle, and the play has assumed such mythic proportions in NFL lore, it's worth wondering just how high Clark really jumped that day. He looks to be fairly climbing the sky. Is the photo misleading us, or is our own aggrandizing of Clark's game-winning catch doing it? If the photographer had shot from a higher angle, or if the touchdown had come in the first half instead of the waning seconds, would we still think of Clark as having leaped out of his shoes that day?

How much is truly in the image, and how much is put there by us? When we look at the photograph on page 19 of Canada's Ben Johnson at the 1988 Olympics in Seoul, we may see a trace of guilt in Johnson's visage as he tears away from the field. But that's only because we know that he tested positive for steroids following the race. Without this knowledge, surely we would see only implacable determination on Johnson's face.

There is indeed more to the picture than meets the eye.

AFTERMATH

Dwight Clark retired from the San Francisco 49ers following the 1987 season, with career totals of 506 receptions, 6,750 yards receiving and 48 touchdowns that reflected nine seasons of solid play. Always a Bay Area favorite, he continued to run his popular restaurant, Clark's-By-The-Bay, in Redwood City. In 1989 he rejoined the 49er organization as a marketing consultant and eventually moved to the front office to work under General Manager John McVay. As his responsibilities with San Francisco increased, Clark sold his restaurant to focus solely on his front-office duties, and in 1994 he was named vice president and director of football operations for the Niners. Precision and concentration, tools that served Clark well on the football field, have been equally useful in negotiating contracts and managing the salary cap.

Joe Montana's pass seemed unreachable, but Dwight Clark, lurking in the very back of the end zone and using every inch of his 6' 4'' frame, stretched skyward to make what has come to be known as "The Catch." The touchdown climaxed a thrilling 89-yard drive that gave the 49ers the 28–27 victory over the Cowboys in the 1981 NFC Championship Game.

The ski jump run
at the 1964
Winter Olympics
offered a
panoramic view
of the city of
Innsbruck, not to
mention the
snow-capped Alps
on the horizon.

Canada's Ben Johnson muscled through the 100-meter event at the 1988 Summer Games, defeating Carl Lewis of the U.S. by .13 of a second and breaking his own world record with a time of 9.79. Johnson's Olympic triumph lasted but a day; when a drug test revealed traces of an anabolic steroid, stanozolol, in his system he was stripped of his gold medal and banned from international competition for two years.

In 1965 Muhammad Ali ended his second encounter with the once-fearsome Sonny Liston much more quickly than his first the year before, flooring Liston in the first round with a seemingly phantom punch, then crowing over his fallen rival.

Minnesota's Dan Gladden knocked Atlanta's Greg Olson upside down on this play in Game 1 of the 1991 World Series, but Olson held on for the out; no matter, the Twins won 5–2 and went on to take the Series in seven games.

For a couple of days, thoughts of the kick never left him. He dragged them back to his hotel room after the game as if they were unruly children who would not keep quiet. There was not much sleep that first night. What could he have done differently? What? The entire kick took 1.3 seconds. It takes as long to say the words—"one-point-three seconds"—as it does to live them. He lived them over and over again. The Bills continually marched up the field, working against the decreasing numbers on the scoreboard clock. He continually kicked into a net, getting loose until he knew he was ready. He stood on the sideline until he was sent into the game. Again and again and again. What could he have changed? He was going on a lifetime of repetition.

—Leigh Montville
Feb. 18, 1991

In arguably the most exciting Super Bowl to date, the Bills' Scott Norwood missed a 47-yard field goal attempt by two feet, preserving the Giants' 20–19 win in Super Bowl XXV.

On June 13, 1948, as part of a celebration of Yankee Stadium's 25th anniversary, a frail Babe Ruth, racked with throat cancer and just two months away from his death, suited up in a Yankee uniform and addressed the New York faithful for the last time.

After a collision with Zola Budd eliminated her from the 3,000-meter Olympic final in 1984, Mary Decker was left in tears over the pain of a pulled gluteus muscle and the regrets of an unfortunate Olympic career: too young in '72; injured in '76; blocked by boycott in '80.

As a native Austrian at the 1976 Winter Games at Innsbruck, Franz Klammer faced intense pressure to win the downhill gold medal; during the last 1,000 meters of the course Klammer made up lost ground to defeat Bernhard Russi of Switzerland by one-third of a second.

No one could
blame Tiger
Woods for pump-
ing a fist or two
after the 1997
Masters. Just
21, Woods had
transformed ven-
erable Augusta
National into a
veritable pitch-
and-putt, shooting
a Masters-record
18-under-par 270
to finish 12
strokes ahead of
his nearest com-
petitor, Tom Kite.

LEADERS
HOLE 1 2 3 4 5 6 7 8 9 10 11 12 13 14 15 16 17 18
PAR 4 5 4 3 4 3 4 5 4 4 4 3 5 4 5 3 4 4
WOODS
ROCCA
STANKOWSKI
KITE T.
WATSON T.
SLUMAN
LOVE
LANGER
COUPLES
TOLLES
THRU 17
WOODS 18
ROCCA 4

In one of the most dramatic endings in World Series history, Pittsburgh's Bill Mazeroski hit a 1–0 pitch from the Yankees' Ralph Terry out of the park in the bottom of the ninth to conclude a Game 7 10–9 slugfest that gave Pittsburgh its first Series title since 1925.

When Bill Skowron ended the Yankee half of the ninth by grounding to [Dick] Groat, Fate truly intervened. Fate's particular Pirate, Bill Mazeroski, came to bat. He had produced the deciding margin in two earlier Pirate victories, with a two-run homer in the first game, which Pittsburgh won 6–4, and a two-run double in the fifth game, which Pittsburgh won 5–2. He let one of Ralph Terry's fastballs go by. Then he hit the next one over the left field fence.

There was noise in Forbes Field then, too, and it went on for more than an hour. Mazeroski took off his cap and swung it around his head as he went leaping and frolicking around the bases. The fans spilled out of their seats and mobbed the Pirates, especially Mazeroski, who had to fight his way to home plate….

It was fitting that the Pirates should win in the ninth and that they should come from behind. The only irony is that the Pittsburgh Pirates beat the New York Yankees with home runs, for the home run is a Yankee weapon, not theirs. But Pittsburgh is a good baseball team, and it makes use of what it has—pitching, defense, line drives to the opposite field. A bit more courage than most, a little more hunger. So why not home runs, too? The important thing is to save them for when they count. The Pirates had been saving those last three for 35 years.

—Roy Terrell
Oct. 24, 1960

Super Bowl V, a.k.a. the "Blunder Bowl," ended mercifully on Jim O'Brien's 32-yard field goal in the closing seconds to give the Colts a 16–13 win over the Cowboys. The game featured a combined six fumbles, six interceptions, a muffed field goal attempt and a blocked PAT.

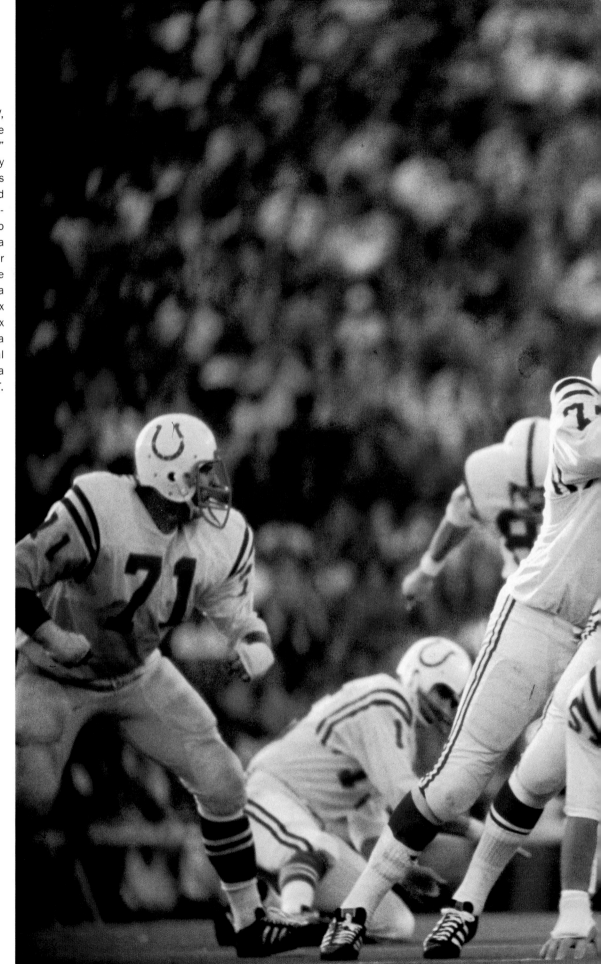

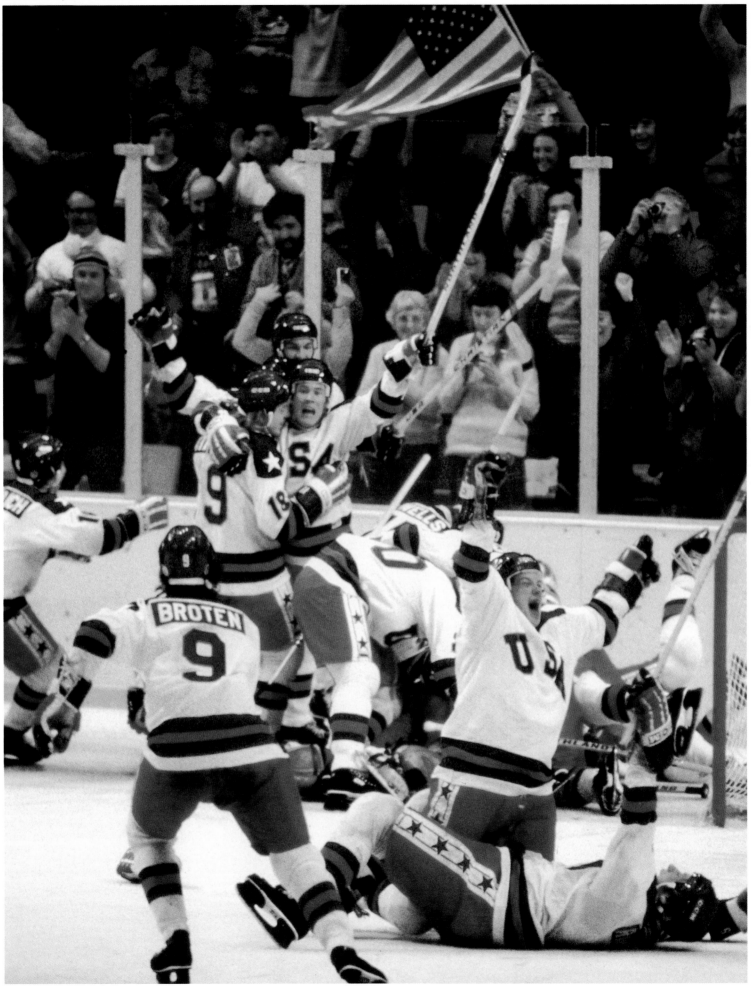

And then it was over. The horn sounded and there was that unforgettable scene of triumph, the rolling and hugging and flinging of sticks. The flags. My God, what a sight. There was the shaking of hands, the staggered, reluctant exit from the ice. But it wasn't until the U.S. players were back in the locker room that the enormity of what they had done hit them. "It was absolutely quiet," recalls [Steve] Janaszak. "Some guys were crying a little. You got the impression that the game wasn't over, because no one is ever up a goal on the Russians when a game is over. No one believed it."

It was then that somebody started a chorus of God Bless America, 20 sweaty guys in hockey uniforms chanting, "… from the mountains, to the valleys, na-na-na-na-na, na-na-na …!" Nobody knew the words. And where was [coach Herb] Brooks? Holed up in the men's room, afraid to come out and ruin their celebration. "I almost started to cry," he says. "It was probably the most emotional moment I'd ever seen. Finally I snuck out into the hall, and the state troopers were all standing there crying. Now where do you go?"

—E.M. Swift
Dec. 22–29, 1980

Miracles do happen: Neal Broten (opposite page) rushed to join the celebration after the U.S. hockey team defeated the Soviets—a feared juggernaut that before the Olympics had defeated the NHL All-Stars and destroyed the Americans in an exhibition game—at the 1980 Winter Olympics in Lake Placid.

Jackie Joyner-Kersee of the U.S. soared to a world-record distance of 24' 3½'' in the women's long jump to win a second gold medal at the 1988 Olympic Games in Seoul. She won her first with a world-record total of 7,291 points in the pentathlon.

As the dust set-
tled in Game 5
of the 1975
World Series,
Pete Rose of the
Reds was tagged
out by Cartlon
Fisk of the Red
Sox. Fisk would
win Game 6 by
seemingly willing
a dramatic home
run into fair terri-
tory in the 12th
inning, but Rose,
who led all
Series batters
with 10 hits, and
Cincinnati would
prevail in Game 7.

Led by innovative coach Paul Brown (right, with tie), the Cleveland Browns of the 1940s and '50s were one of the great dynasties in pro football history, winning four straight AAFC titles before moving to the NFL in 1950 and appearing in six straight title games.

Joan Benoit ran a victory lap around Memorial Coliseum in Los Angeles after winning the first women's marathon in Olympic history in 1984. Her time of 2:24:52 was the third-fastest women's marathon ever.

John Havlicek's dramatic steal in the closing seconds of Game 7 of the 1965 Eastern Conference Finals between Boston and Philadelphia preserved a 110–109 victory for the Celtics.

AFTERMATH

After Havlicek's steal sealed the victory over Philadelphia, the Celtics advanced to the NBA Finals, where they rolled over the Lakers in five games for their seventh straight title. The next season, 1965–66, would mark the end of Boston's string of consecutive championships and Red Auerbach's final year as Celtics coach. By the 1969–70 season Bill Russell, Sam Jones and K.C. Jones were retired, and the Celtic dynasty was finally over.

A pair of titles in the mid-70s revived Boston's hopes but by the late '70s the team was back in the doldrums. Havlicek, one of the last remaining pieces of the '60s dynasty, retired in 1978 as the Celtics' alltime leading scorer (26,395 points), and brought his 20.8 scoring average and eight championship rings to the Hall of Fame in 1983. A 29–53 record in 1978–79 marked the Celtics' nadir, but from the ashes arose not a phoenix but a Bird (Larry), on whose wings Boston again soared to glory in the '80s.

With game-time temperatures plunging to -13°, the 1967 NFL title game between Dallas and Green Bay, which the Packers won on this quarterback sneak by Bart Starr, became known as the "Ice Bowl."

This doubles match at Forest Hills featured the elegant Don Budge (top right), who in addition to winning two U.S. Open doubles titles, in 1938 became the first—and until Rod Laver 24 years later, the only—man to win a Grand Slam.

Record Breakers

Joe DiMaggio's sweet swing often delivered postseason joy to Yankee fans—DiMaggio appeared in 10 World Series and was victorious in nine of them. His legacy also includes one of sport's most unassailable records: his 1941 streak of 56 consecutive games in which he got at least one hit.

Record Breakers

Wilson's mighty swing (opposite) produced a record 190 RBIs in 1930, one of baseball's most venerable milestones.

Records are the spice of the sports world. Champions we crown with almost tiresome regularity, but records fall in unpredictable patterns, often surprising their new owners as much as they do the rest of us.

Look for example at Tony Duffy's head-on shot of an airborne Bob Beamon long jumping at the Mexico City Olympics. What is the expression on Beamon's face? Is it astonishment or routine concentration? How much does Beamon know at this instant? Certainly it looks as if he's just felt some mysterious force lift his body, like the invisible hand of God, but we may interpret his expression that way because we know that he is about to land 29' 2½" away from his launching point, adding an incomprehensible 21¾" to the world record.

Had anyone known that Wilt Chamberlain was going to score 100 points in a routine mid-season game against the New York Knicks, surely there would have been more than 4,124 fans on hand to witness it. And there's no way a renowned bricklayer like Chamberlain could have guessed he'd sink 28 of 32 free throws that night. So there is no film footage of the greatest individual performance in NBA history and no decent photos. But because a titanic struggle was virtually guaranteed every time Chamberlain faced Bill Russell, we have Walter Iooss Jr.'s great photo of Chamberlain grabbing one of his NBA-record 55 rebounds against the Celtics with his rival seemingly cowering between his legs.

As our gallery of record breakers reminds us, there are two types of records, those that measure single, isolated feats—like Beamon's leap—and those measuring sustained greatness, an accretion of feats over a season or career. The latter we all see coming, with the result that we have a fine shot of Pete Rose getting his record-tying 4,191st career hit, of Wayne Gretzky skating to the third of eight straight Hart trophies as league MVP, and of Cal Ripken making an emotional tour of Camden Yards as he shares with fans his finally breaking Lou Gehrig's mark for consecutive games played.

Records put the rest of us in perspective, and it's perspective that makes many of these photos of record breakers so memorable. Check out the ground-level shots of batting-average champ Ty Cobb sliding viciously into third base and of Secretariat pounding his way to a 31-length triumph at Belmont. RBI king Hack Wilson's vicious cut (right) must very nearly have taken off the photographer's head. Mark Spitz is little more than a gasping mouth and single fierce eye as he swims to one of his record seven gold medals at the Munich Olympics in 1972. And there's the great shot of medical student Roger Bannister running history's first four-minute mile. As unforgettable as the picture is for Bannister's obvious effort, the photo is also moving for the reaction of the timers and spectators, on whose faces we see our own amazement mirrored.

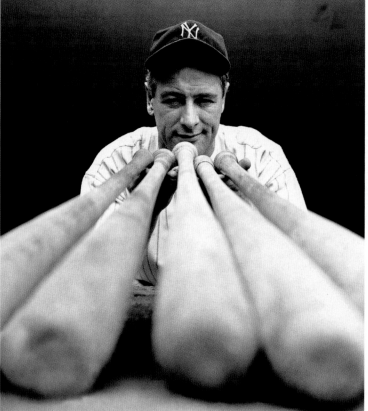

Perhaps because Lou Gehrig played most of his career in the shadow of Babe Ruth, many of his accomplishments, other than his streak of 2,130 consecutive games, are often forgotten: an AL-record 184 RBIs in 1931; 13 straight years of 100 runs and 100 RBIs; and, in 1934, astonishing Triple Crown numbers: a .363 average, 49 home runs and 165 RBIs.

The man with whom Gehrig will forever be linked in history is Baltimore's classy Cal Ripken Jr., who broke Gehrig's consecutive-game streak in 1997 and provoked a nationwide celebration of Ripken's character as much as his style of play. Ripken ran his streak to 2,632 games before gracefully deciding to sit one out on Sept. 20, 1998.

Before joining pro football's Canton Bulldogs in 1915, the legendary Jim Thorpe, who also played pro baseball, obliterated the Olympic record in the decathlon at the 1912 Games in Stockholm. His performance would still have earned a silver medal at the 1948 Olympics.

Powered by his 27-inch thighs, Eric Heiden (opposite page) became the first athlete to win five individual gold medals during a single Olympics, triumphing in the 500-, 1,000-, 1500-, 5,000- and 10,000-meter speed skating races at Lake Placid in 1980.

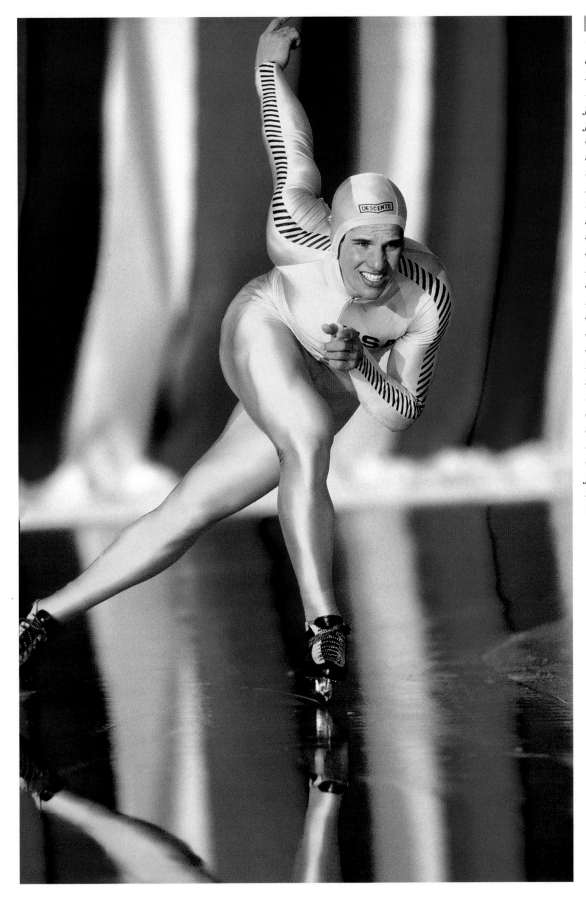

"The 1980 Games seem like a lifetime ago," speed skater Eric Heiden told Sports Illustrated in 1998. But when he crossed the finish line in first place after his final race in Lake Placid, Heiden believed he had reached the pinnacle of his life. Turns out he was just beginning his ascent. Following the Games Heiden went on to complete graduate study at Stanford University, compete as a world-class cyclist, and graduate from Stanford's Medical School. Now an orthopedic surgeon, he practices at UC-Davis in Sacramento, where he often performs four or five surgeries a day. "I'm really more concerned with being the best doctor I can be and being respected by my peers, being known for more than skating a couple of laps around a rink faster than anyone else," he told SI. Thus, he keeps his five gold medals far from his office, and is unperturbed by the fact that some of his patients know nothing of his glorious Olympic past.

In only his third marathon, the barefoot Abebe Bikila of Ethiopia, a member of Haile Selassie's Imperial Body-guard, broke the world record at the 1960 Olympics in Rome, crossing the finish line at the Arch of Constantine with a time of 2:15:16.2.

The intensely competitive Ty Cobb made any infielder who dared obstruct his path pay for such audacity; before his brilliant 24-year career was over Cobb had 4,191 hits, more than any player in history, a record that stood 57 years until Pete Rose surpassed it in 1985.

In 1962, Rod Laver joined Don Budge as the only two men in tennis history who have won Grand Slams, but the Rocket stands a cut above the great Budge for having turned the difficult trick twice. He won his second Slam in '69, dominating the circuit with 31 consecutive victories.

San Francisco treat: Few dispute that the 49ers' Jerry Rice is the greatest receiver of all time. He has more catches for more yards and more touchdowns than any receiver in league history; he has three Super Bowl rings and one Super Bowl MVP award—and, if there are still any doubters, he's not done yet.

Afield, as in life, Rice is evasive. He almost never takes a direct, crushing blow after catching a pass. He controls his body like a master puppeteer working a marionette. A one-handed grab here, a tiptoe up the sideline there, an unscathed sprint through two closing safeties when it seems decapitation is imminent.

"I don't think I've ever seen him all stretched out," says 49er quarterback Steve Young of Rice's ability to avoid big hits. Rice jumps only when he has to, and unlike almost all other receivers, he catches passes in mid-stride and effortlessly continues running, the ball like a sprinter's baton in his hand. It's almost certain that no one has run for more yardage after catching the ball than Rice. Though he's not particularly fast, Rice has a fluid stride and sudden burst that, as Young says, "is a speed you can't clock."

—Rick Telander
Dec. 26, 1994

Michael Johnson, who had won the 400 meters earlier in the 1996 Atlanta Games, completed the first successful 200/400 double in Olympic history with a flourish, crossing the 200-meter finish line in 19.32 to shatter the world record by .34 seconds.

In 1970, free-skating Bobby Orr led the Boston Bruins to their first Stanley Cup title since 1941 and transformed his position by becoming the first defenseman ever to lead the NHL in scoring. In an era when a 20-goal season was unheard of for a defenseman, Orr scored 33 goals and passed off for 87 assists. His 135 points in 1975 is still the highest total for a defenseman.

In the summer of 1984, after five seasons in Philadelphia and a brief stint in Montreal, Pete Rose returned to the Cincinnati Reds as player-manager. What seemed like the perfect ending to a storied career did not stay that way for long. By spring training of the 1989 season, Rose, now a full-time manager, was being investigated by Major League Baseball for his associations with convicted felons and allegations that he had placed illegal bets, some of them on baseball games. As if that weren't enough, he was also under investigation by a Cincinnati grand jury for possible tax evasion in conjunction with autograph signings and memorabilia sales. It all came crashing down around Rose in late August of that year. He was banned from baseball for life by commissioner Bart Giamatti for what Giamatti termed "engaging in a variety of acts which have stained the game." Rose was later convicted of and served jail time for tax evasion. While he acknowledged much wrongdoing, Rose never admitted to gambling on baseball games. As of 1998 baseball's alltime hits leader remained banned from the game and excluded from the Hall of Fame.

Johnny Weissmuller, later known as the silver screen's original Tarzan, set 51 swimming world records at distances ranging from 50 to 800 meters; he also won a total of five gold medals in the 1924 and '28 Olympics.

Answer: The Cubs' Reggie Patterson. Question: Who gave up Pete Rose's 4,191st career hit in 1985, a line drive to right field that tied him with Ty Cobb atop the alltime major league hit list?

Bobby Hull, a.k.a. the Golden Jet, broke the single-season goals record of 50 he had shared with Maurice Richard and Bernie Geoffrion when he fired home his 51st goal—in just his 61st game of the year—against the Rangers in 1966.

Facing Bill Russell and the defending champion Celtics on Nov. 24, 1960, Wilt Chamberlain pulled down 55 rebounds, still an NBA record. Chamberlain would set another—and perhaps even more untouchable—mark in 1962 when he scored 100 points against the New York Knicks.

Jesse Owens, the son of Alabama sharecoppers, won four track and field gold medals—in the 100 meters, the 200, the long jump and the 4 x 100-meter relay—at the 1936 Olympics in Berlin; one year earlier, during the Big Ten championship meet in Ann Arbor, Mich., Owens had achieved international renown by breaking five world records and tying a sixth in the space of just 45 minutes.

Secretariat was an amiable, gentlemanly colt, with a poised and playful nature that at times made him seem as much a pet as the stable dog was. I was standing in front of his stall one morning, writing, when he reached out, grabbed my notebook in his teeth and sank back inside, looking to see what I would do. "Give the man his notebook back!" yelled [groom Eddie] Sweat. As the groom dipped under the webbing, Secretariat dropped the notebook on the bed of straw....

By his personality and temperament, Secretariat became the most engaging character in the barn. His own stable pony, a roan named Billy Silver, began an unrequited love affair with him. "He loves Secretariat, but Secretariat don't pay any attention to him," Sweat said one day. "If Billy sees you grazin' Secretariat, he'll go to hollerin' until you bring him out. Secretariat just ignores him. Kind of sad, really."

—William Nack
June 4, 1990

After winning the 1973 Kentucky Derby in record time and taking the Preakness by 2½ lengths, Secretariat ran away with the Belmont by 31 lengths to remove any doubts about his place in history. The colt covered the 1½ miles in 2:24, still the fastest time ever for that distance, becoming the ninth Triple Crown winnner in history and the first since Citation in 1948.

At the rate the long jump record had progressed to that point—8¼ inches in 33 years—Bob Beamon's world record leap of 29' 2½" at the 1968 Olympics in Mexico City, which added 21¾ inches to the record, was roughly half a century ahead of its time. Indeed, the next jump of more than 28 feet—a barrier Beamon sprang past entirely—would not occur until 1980.

In 1982, in just his third season, Wayne Gretzky broke his own single-season scoring record with 212 points on 92 goals and 120 assists, a record he later broke again, with a 215-point season in 1986. The eight-time league MVP passed another milestone in 1994 when his 802nd goal moved him past Gordie Howe as the all-time NHL career leader in goals scored.

On May 6, 1954, at Iffley Road track in Oxford, Roger Bannister of England achieved one of the twentieth century's sporting benchmarks, running a mile in 3:59.4 to break the four-minute barrier. *Sports Illustrated,* which launched in 1954, named Bannister its first Sportsman of the Year.

Swimmer Mark Spitz secured a permanent place in the pantheon of Olympic heroes when he won an unprecedented—and since unequaled—seven gold medals at the Summer Games in Munich. Spitz set world records in each of the four individual events he entered—the 100- and 200-meter freestyles, and the 100- and 200-meter butterflies—and was a member of three gold medal–winning relay teams.

The elegant Hank Aaron never had a 50-homer season during his 23 year career, but his relentless consistency—he hit 30 home runs or more in 15 of 17 seasons in one stretch—finally brought him what he called the Cadillac of home run records when his 715th home run, off the Dodgers' Al Downing in 1974, moved him past Babe Ruth and into first on the alltime home run list.

For those who sat in the stadium in Atlanta, their recollections would be more intimate—the sharp, cork-popping sound of the bat hitting the ball, startlingly audible in the split second of suspense before the crowd began a roar that lasted for more than 10 minutes. Perhaps that is what they would remember—how people stood in front of their seats and sucked in air and bellowed it out in a sustained tribute that few athletes have ever received. Or perhaps they would remember their wonder at how easy and inevitable it seemed—that having opened the season in Cincinnati by hitting the tying home run, No. 714, with his first swing of the year, it was obviously appropriate that the man who has been called Supe by his teammates (for Superman) was going to duplicate the feat in Atlanta with his first swing of *that* game. That was why 53,775 had come. Or perhaps they would remember the odd way the stadium emptied after the excitement of the fourth inning, as if the crowd felt that what they had seen would be diluted by sitting through any more baseball that night."

—George Plimpton
April 22, 1974

Bob Mathias was only 17 when he competed in the Olympic decathlon at the London Games in 1948 and became the youngest winner of a men's track and field event in the history of the Games; four years later, in Helsinki, he made more history as the first man to win back-to-back decathlon gold medals.

Jack Nicklaus made a splash in the world of golf at an early age, winning the U.S. Amateur in 1959 and '61 as a student at Ohio State before taking the PGA by storm; by the time he left for the Senior Tour in 1990, Nicklaus had won a total of 20 majors—18 of them of the professional variety—to set a standard that may never be equaled.

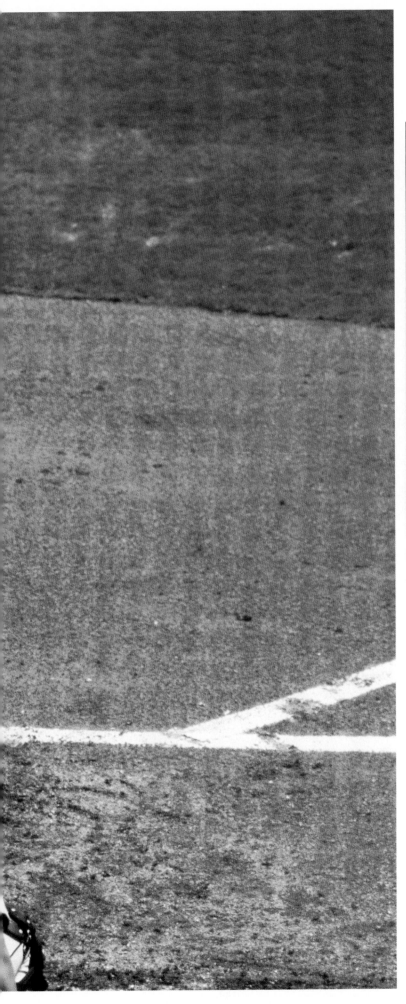

While no one will ever surpass the legend of Babe Ruth (above), who more or less invented the home run as a member of the Yankees in the 1920s, Cardinals slugger Mark McGwire (left) accomplished two things in 1998 that no player, including the Sultan of Swat, had ever done: He belted 70 homers on the year, and completed his third straight season with at least 50 home runs.

The Big Events

Representatives of the Green Bay Packers (right) and the Kansas City Chiefs met at midfield for the coin toss before the first Super Bowl in the Los Angeles Memorial Coliseum on Jan. 15, 1967. Green Bay defended the honor of the NFL establishment by defeating the AFL champions 35–10.

Big Events

The biggest events do not necessarily yield the best photos. Those end-of-season, do-or-die clashes between dominant teams or individuals will always generate tremendous interest, for they are moments of real reckoning, and such moments are rare in sport and in life. But they do not guarantee great photos, which depend more on the quirks of body positioning, facial expression and lighting than on the importance of the contest. That said, big events can yield great pictures, and often do, as this gallery of championship photos so eloquently reminds us.

Some are well known but breathtaking all the same, like the shot of Willie Mays's back as he runs down Vic Wertz's long drive in the 1954 World Series and the top of Alan Ameche's helmet as he plunges over the goal line in what many consider to be the greatest pro football game of all time, the Baltimore Colts' 23–17 overtime win over the New York Giants in the 1958 NFL title game.

There are countless reasons why the picture of Montreal Canadiens goalie Jacques Plante is memorable. To start with, photographer John G. Zimmerman has caught the precise moment when the other players have parted like the Red Sea, leaving a narrow lane of empty ice that frames Plante perfectly. Note too the contrast between the utter concentration on Plante's face and the expressions on the faces of the spectators behind him, who, while intrigued, are one step removed from the action. The photo is also interesting for historical reasons. The next year Plante revo-

lutionized goaltending by wearing a mask.

Our gallery shows us moments of elation: legendary Green Bay Packer coach Vince Lombardi perched atop the shoulders of guard Jerry Kramer after Green Bay's 33–14 win over the Oakland Raiders in Super Bowl II; and Yogi Berra leaping into Don Larsen's arms after Larsen pitched the only perfect game in World Series history.

Photographers go where we can't; for example, along the baseline of the 1966 NCAA title game in which all-black Texas Western upset a heavily-favored all-white Kentucky team that included future NBA coach Pat Riley *(42, right)*. Elsewhere, using a camera mounted on the backboard, photographer Manny Millan shows us Julius Erving soaring in for a basket over the outstretched arm of Kareem Abdul-Jabbar in the 1983 NBA Finals. The great Dr. J, who scored seven points in a 98-second span of Game 4, must have been hot, since the photo reveals what television couldn't: Erving is not even looking at the basket.

And speaking of places fans can't go, take a look at the great photo of fans milling around on the field at the Huntington Avenue Baseball Grounds in Boston *before* the first-ever World Series game, in 1903. In this game the Pirates would beat the Boston Pilgrims of the upstart American League 7–3, but the Pilgrims would come back to take the best-of-nine Series five games to three. It's just about impossible to get down on the field these days, but thanks to great photography we really don't have to.

The Doctor is in: Julius Erving and the Philadelphia 76ers found the right prescription to avenge two NBA championship defeats by the Los Angeles Lakers in three seasons, sweeping L.A. in 1983. In Game 4 Erving scored seven points in a 98-second span as Philadelphia clinched its first title in 16 years with a 115–108 win.

New York's Willie Mays's stunning over-the-shoulder catch of a drive by Cleveland's Vic Wertz in Game 1 of the 1954 World Series is arguably baseball's most famous out. Taking off from left center field with the crack of the bat, Mays sprinted to right center and latched onto Wertz's blast in stride, 460 feet from home plate. The Giants went on to sweep the favored Indians.

Coach Vince Lombardi received a victory ride from guard Jerry Kramer following the Green Bay Packers' 33–14 romp over Oakland in Super Bowl II. Lombardi, whose Packers won Super Bowl I as well, retired after the victory; the trophy now awarded to Super Bowl winners bears his name.

The fearsome threesome of Lawrence Taylor (top), Jim Burt (64) and Carl Banks (58) led the Giants defense, which produced an interception, four sacks and a safety in New York's 39–20 victory over Denver in Super Bowl XXI.

When Sonny Liston was unable to answer the bell for Round 7 during his 1964 title fight, the celebration began for manager Angelo Dundee (right) and the new heavyweight champion of the world, Cassius Clay, who would soon change his name to Muhammad Ali. The budding legend celebrated in his signature brash style: part clown, part provocateur, part witness to his own greatness.

With his team trailing the upstart New York Jets 16–0 in Super Bowl III, the 35-year-old Johnny Unitas rallied Baltimore to a fourth-quarter touchdown but was unable to orchestrate a comeback as the heavily favored Colts became the first NFL team to lose a Super Bowl.

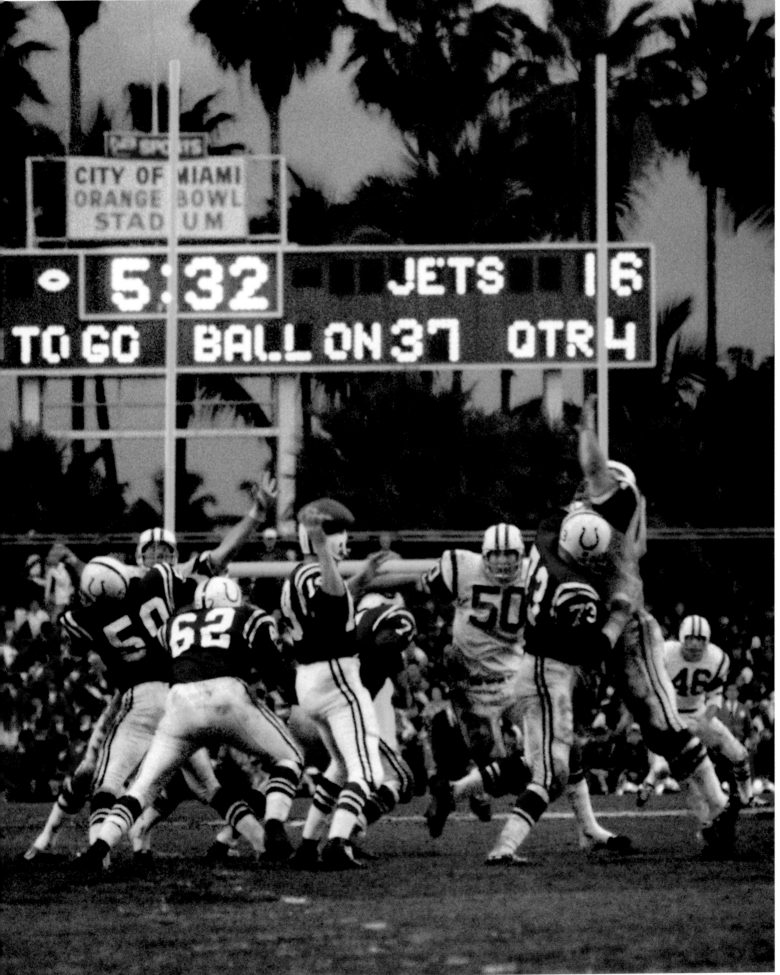

CITY OF MIAMI
ORANGE BOWL
STADIUM

5:32 JETS 16
TO GO BALL ON 37 QTR 4

New York's Tommie Agee (20) was one major reason the amazing Mets upset Jim Palmer and the heavily favored Baltimore Orioles in Game 3 of the 1969 World Series; Agee hit a lead-off homer, then made a pair of sensational catches in center field which may have saved the Mets as many as five runs.

In 1984, for the second straight year, Martina Navratilova defeated Chris Evert at the U.S. Open; the 4–6, 6–4, 6–4 win was Navratilova's 13th straight defeat of Evert, her archrival for nearly a decade.

Darryl Johnston and the Dallas Cowboys' running game hit repeated roadblocks against the Pittsburgh Steelers in the second half of Super Bowl XXX; Dallas needed two interceptions from game MVP Larry Brown to produce the two touchdowns that nailed down the 27–17 Dallas win.

Daniel Passarella, the captain of Argentina's national soccer team, received a victory ride from the adoring home crowd at River Plate Stadium after Argentina's 3–1 overtime win against Holland in the 1978 World Cup Final.

He hit just .225 with five home runs during the regular season, but in the 1972 World Series Gene Tenace was a powerhouse, ripping a pair of homers in his first two at-bats in Oakland's 3–2 Game 1 win over the Cincinnati Reds.

AFTERMATH

The 1903 World Series match between Pittsburgh and Boston was made after years of ill will between the established National League and the fledgling American League. The tenuous bond between the rival circuits was broken the very next year when John McGraw, manager of the NL champion New York Giants, refused to play the Pilgrims, who had repeated as AL titlists, saying, "We are the champions of the only real major league."

McGraw's stubbornness caused a one-year Series hiatus—not to be repeated until the dread strike year 1994—but the New York skipper relented in 1905, and the World Series was officially and permanently established. His Giants met the AL champion Philadelphia Athletics in that Series and won, four games to one, as pitcher Christy Mathewson threw three shutouts. The national game had its centerpiece, and the Golden Age of baseball was underway.

Fans converged on Boston's Huntington Avenue Grounds before the opening game of the first World Series on Oct. 1, 1903. Armed with a pitcher named Cy Young, the Boston Pilgrims of the upstart American League went on to defeat the Pittsburgh Pirates of the more established National League, five games to three.

Troy Aikman and the Dallas Cowboys leapt—nay, steamrolled—over the Buffalo Bills in Super Bowl XXVII in Pasadena. Aikman, who threw for 273 yards and four touchdowns, was named MVP in the Cowboys' 52–17 victory, the third-most lopsided in Super Bowl history.

New York's Don Larsen and Yogi Berra (8) were joy incarnate after Larsen completed the only perfect game in World Series history in Game 5 of the 1956 Fall Classic against the Brooklyn Dodgers.

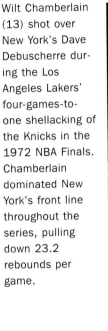

Wilt Chamberlain (13) shot over New York's Dave Debuscherre during the Los Angeles Lakers' four-games-to-one shellacking of the Knicks in the 1972 NBA Finals. Chamberlain dominated New York's front line throughout the series, pulling down 23.2 rebounds per game.

Montreal's Jacques Plante was peerless in goal for the Canadiens in 1958, leading the NHL with a stingy goals-against average of 2.11. He would revolutionize his position the following year by introducing the goalie mask to the NHL.

Alan Ameche dived into the end zone with the game-winning touchdown in overtime as the Baltimore Colts defeated the New York Giants 23–17 for the 1958 NFL championship; the game, the first to be televised nationally, would come to be known as pro football's greatest.

The Baltimore Colts needed all their varied and impressive talent to get the 17–17 tie at the end of the regular four quarters. Then, for eight and one quarter minutes of the sudden-death extra period, in which victory would go to the first team to score, all of the pressure and all of the frenzy of an entire season of play was concentrated on the misty football field at Yankee Stadium. The fans kept up a steady high roar. Tension grew and grew until it was nearly unbearable. But on the field itself, where the two teams now staked the pro championship and a personal winner's share of $4,700 against a loser's share of $3,100 on each play, coldly precise football prevailed. With each team playing as well as it was possible for it to play, the better team finally won. The Colts, ticking off the yards with sure strength under the magnificent direction of quarterback Johnny Unitas, scored the touchdown that brought sudden death to New York and the first championship to hungry Baltimore.

—Tex Maule
Jan. 5, 1959

UCLA's Lew Alcindor—later Kareem Abdul-Jabbar—showcased the awesome weapon which would come to be called the Skyhook as the Bruins rolled over Elvin Hayes (44) and Houston 101–69 in the semifinal round of the 1968 NCAA tournament.

Cheryl Miller graduated from USC in 1986, two years after leading the U.S. Olympic team in scoring, rebounding, steals and assists as the U.S. cruised to the gold medal in Los Angeles. In 1993 Miller returned to her alma mater as the women's basketball coach and one year later guided the Women of Troy to the NCAA regional finals. Uncomfortable in the glare of the media spotlight at USC, she resigned the following season. In 1996 she became the first female analyst to call a nationally televised NBA game, and the following year, the inaugural season of the WNBA, she joined the new women's league as head coach of the Phoenix Mercury. In 1995 Miller was inducted into the Basketball Hall of Fame.

Freshman Cheryl Miller put up incredible numbers—27 points, four blocked shots, four steals and nine rebounds—while leading USC to a 69–67 victory over defending champion Louisiana Tech in the 1983 NCAA championship game.

As was his custom, Sugar Ray Robinson worked the body in a 1957 bout against frequent opponent Gene Fullmer. Robinson won the fight to earn the middleweight title for the fourth time in his illustrious career.

Tennessee's Daedra Charles drove past Virginia's Heidi Burge for two points in the Vols' 70–67 victory over the Cavaliers in the 1991 NCAA championship game; it was Tennessee's third NCAA title in five seasons.

Averaging an unheard-of 29.9 rebounds per game in the playoffs, Boston center Bill Russell led the Celtics to their third consecutive NBA title in 1961 as they defeated the St. Louis Hawks in five games.

Larry Csonka rumbled for 112 yards as the Miami Dolphins completed an unprecedented 17–0 season with a 14–7 victory over Washington in Super Bowl VII.

Jesse Orosco hurled his glove heavenward as if in tribute to the gods for the Mets' Game 7 victory over Boston in the 1986 World Series. New York had been one strike away from losing the series in Game 6 until several clutch Mets hits and Mookie Wilson's infamous ground ball between Bill Buckner's legs gave New York a 6–5 win.

Chicago's Michael Jordan took his game even higher in the 1993 NBA Finals, averaging 41 points, 8.5 rebounds and 6.3 assists per game in the Bulls' six-game series win over Phoenix.

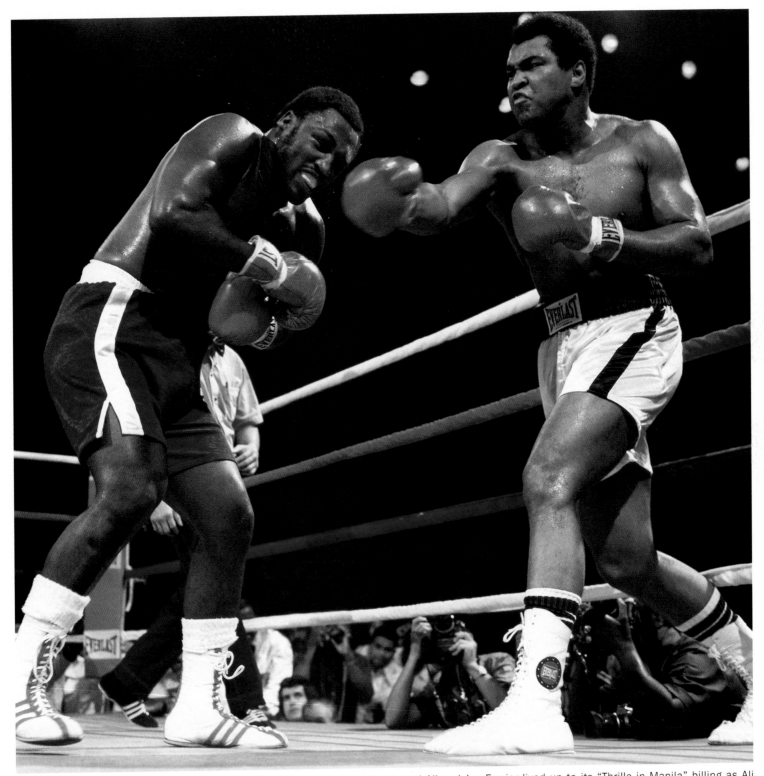

The third installment in the epic series of confrontations between Muhammad Ali and Joe Frazier lived up to its "Thrilla in Manila" billing as Ali went to his seemingly inexhaustible supply of courage and summoned one last surge to batter Frazier into defenselessness in the later rounds.

Pittsburgh's Lynn Swann made four acrobatic catches in the Steelers' 21–17 Super Bowl X victory over Dallas, including this juggling grab at midfield as he fell over Cowboys defender Mark Washington. His game totals: 161 yards, one touchdown and one MVP award.

Athletes

The aerial
artistry of
Michael Jordan
probably evoked
more awe-struck
gasps from fans
fortunate enough
to witness his
play than any
other spectacle
in sports history.

Athletes

West (opposite page), one of the NBA's most reliable performers in the clutch during his 14 seasons with the Lakers, possessed an effortless grace that seemed to belie the intense work ethic he brought to the game.

Athletes inhabit a world of constant motion, where one instant flows without pause into the next. To arrest that flow in a still photo is in some ways to falsify experience, but it certainly makes for some wonderful images, the details of which we can savor in a way we never could at full speed. The split-second acrobatics displayed by Larry Bird as he snares a ball with his right hand while balancing his body on his left are a wonder to behold, as is the intensity of a sliding Pete Rose or a fireballing Bob Gibson.

If our photo of Jerry West driving to the hoop at right looks familiar, it is probably due to the fact that the NBA has been using his silhouette on its logo for the past quarter-century. While not as iconic as the photo of West or indeed the aerial shot of Michael Jordan soaring to the hoop, the other pictures in our collection of great athletes reveal their subjects in startling ways both on and off the field.

Our eyes are drawn to the subjects' eyes. Pete Sampras's eyes smolder with predatory intensity as he rushes the ball. Bill Russell and Wilt Chamberlain, rival centers for the ages, might as well be waiting for the heavens to part and God to show his face, so intent are they as they wait for a rebound. And Magic Johnson, who probably played basketball with more zest than anyone before or after him, is wide-eyed as he starts down court, instantly taking stock of his many options.

Perhaps because we are used to seeing them in action, there is something arresting about the sight of an athlete in repose. The great pitcher Satchel Paige wears a look of weary melancholy as he sits outside the dugout, and Pittsburgh shortstop Honus Wagner takes a moment to contemplate the tools of the hitter's trade. Tennis player Arthur Ashe was always the model of gentlemanly seriousness, as our picture of him reading suggests.

There are also moments of joy, expressed here by Herma Planck-Szabo, the 1924 Olympic figure skating champion, and by Carl Lewis as he anchors the U.S. to a gold medal and a world record in the 4 x 100 relay at the Barcelona Olympics of 1992. Still, as palpable as is Lewis's joy, we are moved at least as much by the faces of the pair of relatively unknown anchormen behind him who may have lost the race but clearly felt a sense of triumph.

Finally, our gallery of athletes includes pictures of two stars who were almost as famous for their shenanigans off the field as for their performance on it. In Walter Iooss Jr.'s picture of a smiling Joe Namath, round-the-clock playboy and Sunday afternoon quarterback, we find Namath soaking up sun and adoration at poolside in (then) fashionable plaid swim trunks. The picture of moon-faced Babe Ruth, smiling sheepishly in the midst of a small army of children, is a sweet reminder of Ruth's love for children and of the years he himself spent in a Baltimore home for boys. It is a wonderful counterpoint to the more famous shot of a dying Ruth, stoop-shouldered and bent by cancer, at Yankee Stadium in 1948.

Pittsburgh short-stop Honus Wagner, one of baseball's first true stars, hit .300 or better 15 seasons in a row; in perhaps his finest hour, he outhit and stole more bases than Ty Cobb while helping the Pirates defeat Cobb's Tigers in seven games for the 1909 World Series title.

AFTERMATH

When recurring back problems forced the legendary Larry Bird to call it quits after 13 seasons, it was a safe bet that the NBA had not seen the last of him. In 1993, he accepted a vaguely defined "special assistant" job with the Boston Celtics, in which he functioned mostly as a consultant. But the position never expanded to the more prominent front-office role he sought. In 1997 he accepted the job as head coach of the Indiana Pacers. Since Bird was a native of French Lick, Indiana, the move made sense geographically, and perhaps sentimentally, but otherwise the decision was a bit of a surprise. As it turned out, the surprise was on those who doubted Bird's abilities to cope with the athletes of the '90s. He guided the Pacers to 58 regular-season wins and Game 7 of the Eastern Conference finals, where they lost to the eventual champion Chicago Bulls after a tough series. For his efforts, the rookie coach was named NBA Coach of the Year.

Larry Bird combined natural talent with a relentless work ethic to add three more championship banners to the crowded Boston Garden rafters during the 1980s.

At the 1992 Olympics in Barcelona, Carl Lewis ran a blistering anchor leg to bring the U.S. 4 x 100-meter relay team home in a world record time of 37.40 and win his eighth Olympic gold medal.

Baltimore third baseman Brooks Robinson made the 1970 World Series a near one-man show, rendering defensive plays like this one routine and rapping out nine hits, including two homers, as the Orioles defeated the Cincinnati Reds in five games to erase the memory of their loss to the underdog Mets the previous year.

Graceful Herma Planck-Szabo of Austria won the women's figure skating competition at the inaugural Winter Olympics in Chamonix in 1924; perhaps more notable was the eighth-place finish of 11-year-old Sonja Henie of Norway, who would take the gold at the next three Winter Games.

Johnny Podres of the world champion Brooklyn Dodgers received a hero's welcome in his hometown, the small mining village of Witherbee, New York, following his brilliant performance in the Dodgers' defeat of the New York Yankees in the 1955 World Series.

Today, even the dream is different. It does not deal with beggar boys becoming kings, or knights on white chargers. The boy kicks a football along Gorky Street and imagines himself booting the winning goal for Spartak in Dynamo Stadium in Moscow. He belts a hurley ball along the rich turf with a stick of Irish ash and thinks how grand it would be in Corke Park in Dublin saving the All-Ireland title for Cork. He stands on the edge of a street in a village in Provence as the Tour de France wheels by and sees himself pedaling into Parc des Princes Stadium in Paris, miles ahead of Louison Bobet. He throws a ball against the battered side of a house and dreams of pitching Brooklyn to victory in the World Series....

And so, when the country boy from the small mining village stands alone on the mound in Yankee Stadium in the most demanding moment of one of the world's few truly epic sports events, and courageously, skillfully pitches his way to a success as complete, melodramatic and extravagant as that ever dreamed by any boy, the American chapter of the International Order of Frustrated Dreamers rises as one man and roars its recognition.

—Robert Creamer
Jan. 2, 1956

Franco Harris spearheaded the Steelers' running attack in the 1970s, rushing for 354 yards and four touchdowns in Pittsburgh's four Super Bowl victories. His MVP-winning performance against the Vikings in Super Bowl IX produced a then-record 158 yards on 34 carries.

While Chicago's six NBA titles in eight seasons in the '90s owe much to the incomparable brilliance of Michael Jordan (23), supporting players such as rebounder extraordinaire Dennis Rodman (right) and jump-shooter Steve Kerr (25) completed the championship puzzle.

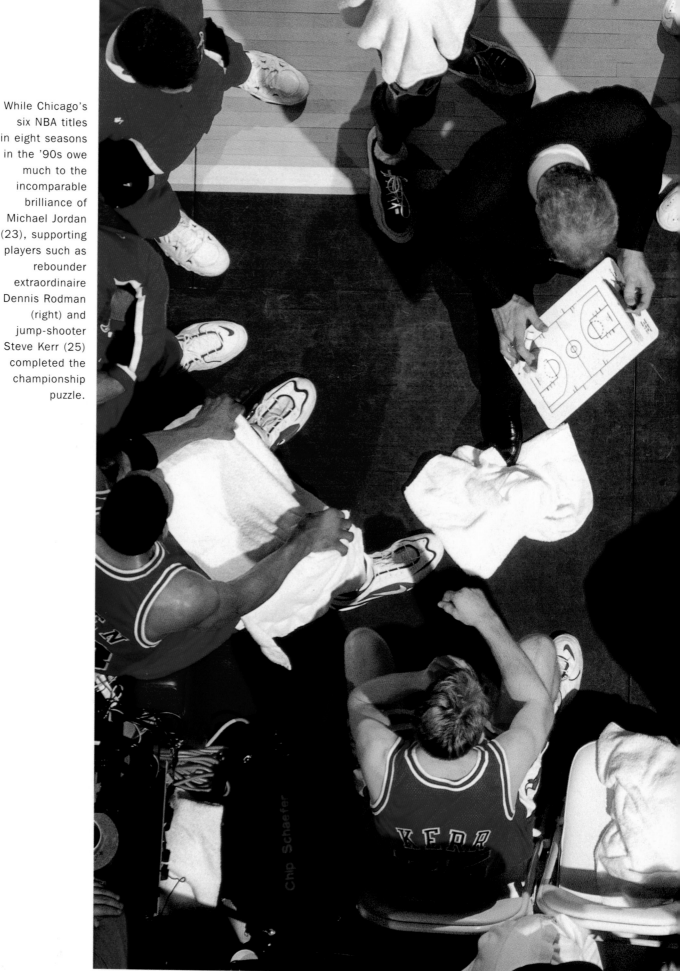

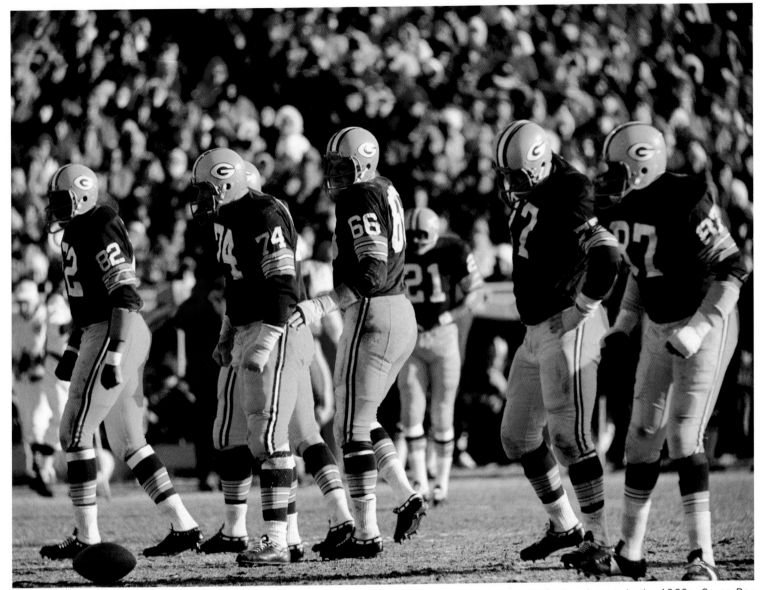

With Ray Nitschke (66) as its snarling centerpiece, the Green Bay defense was the foundation of the Packer dynasty in the 1960s. Green Bay won five NFL titles in the decade, including the first two Super Bowls, and Nitschke was named MVP of the '62 NFL championship game.

Johnny Bench, perhaps the greatest catcher of all time, was the biggest cog in the Big Red Machine's sweep of the Yankees in 1976, batting .533 for the Series and driving in five runs in the deciding Game 4.

Joe Cool: Perhaps the most memorable of Joe Montana's many game-winning, high-blood-pressure-inducing drives came in Super Bowl XXIII, when he guided the 49ers on a 92-yard march for the decisive score against the Bengals, completing eight passes along the way, including the clinching 10-yarder to John Taylor with 39 seconds left.

IN SI's WORDS

Montana loves to watch replays of The Drive, that 92-yard march in Miami's Joe Robbie Stadium that beat the Bengals, 20–16, in the final 3:10 of Super Bowl XXIII last year. He can't remember it any other way. "It's a blur," Montana says. "I hyperventilated to the point of almost blacking out. You know how a TV screen gets fuzzy? Well that's what my vision was like. I was yelling so loudly in the huddle that I couldn't breathe. Things got blurrier and blurrier.

"One time, I put my hands under center and I felt like it was taking days to call the play. Everything was in slow motion. When I took my first step back, the fuzz appeared again. By the fifth step, things got so fuzzy I had to throw the ball over Jerry Rice, out of bounds, to clear my head."

—Jill Lieber
Jan. 29, 1990

Cincinnati's Pete Rose knew only one way to approach the game of baseball: at full speed. Is it any wonder that he earned the nickname "Charlie Hustle?"

Bill Russell (left) and his Celtics defeated Wilt Chamberlain's teams in seven of eight playoff series, but make no mistake, the rivalry between the two big men was the most titanic in NBA history; Chamberlain supporters will cite Russell's superior supporting cast as the reason for Boston's lopsided advantage.

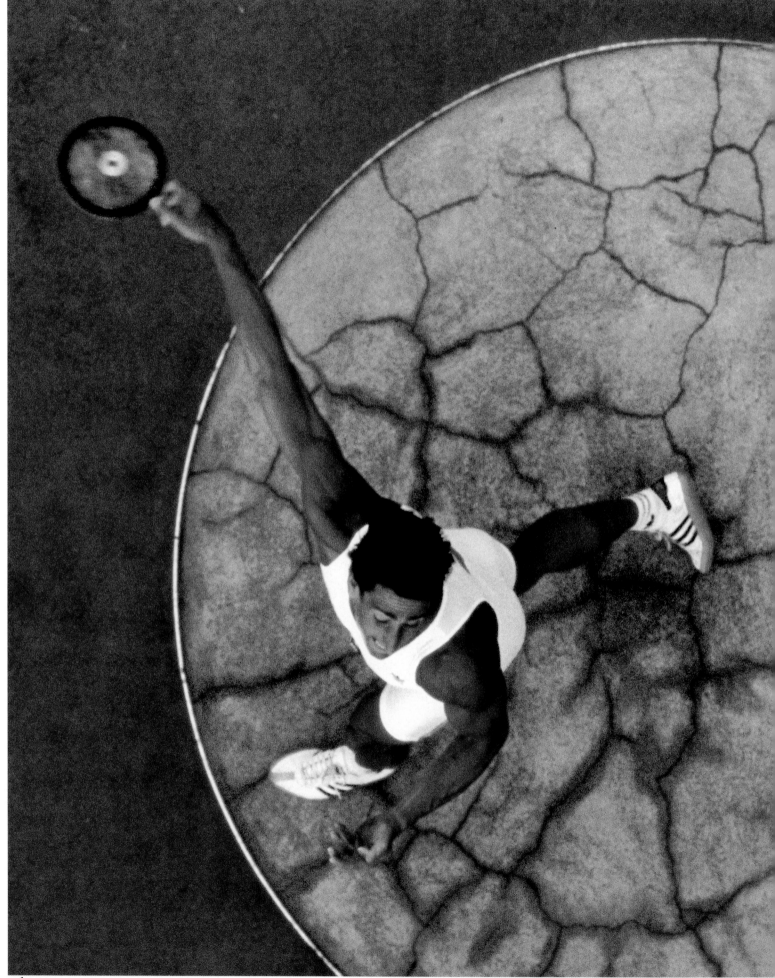

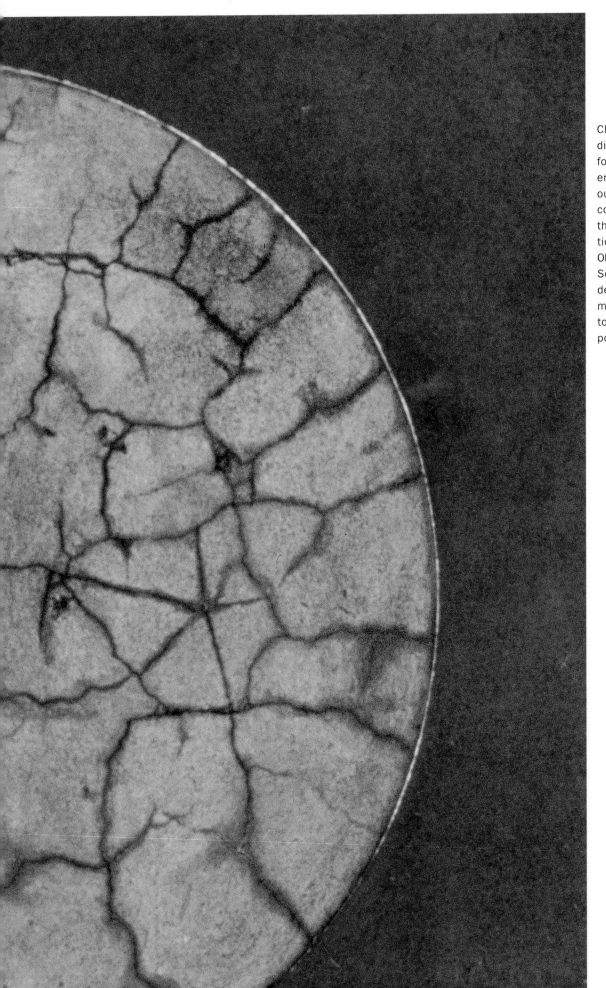

Christian Schenk displayed the form that enabled him to outdistance his competition in the discus portion of the 1988 Olympic decathlon; Schenk won the decathlon gold medal with a total of 8,488 points.

Thumbs up: Even unflappable film critic Gene Siskel (front row center, in black shirt) was awed by Dennis Rodman's all-out effort to reach the basketball at any cost. Rodman's rebounding mastery was a major factor in the Bulls' second NBA title three-peat from 1996 to '98.

Pittsburgh's legendary Steel Curtain defense, whose members included L.C. Greenwood (68), Mean Joe Greene (75) and Dwight White (78), formed the backbone of four Steeler championship teams in the 1970s.

Although he knew a million ways to score, Gordie Howe (9) was hardly a finesse-only player. While scoring 801 goals in his 26 NHL seasons Howe rarely missed an opportunity to inflict punishment on an opponent, and the boards were a favorite ally in this endeavor.

The menacing Bob Gibson liked to work a fast game, and the numbers piled up quickly during his 17-year career with St. Louis. He enjoyed five 20-win seasons, seven consecutive World Series complete-game victories and one of the best pitching seasons ever, in 1968: 1.12 ERA, 268 strikeouts, 13 shutouts.

A relaxed Billie Jean King awaited her "Battle of the Sexes" with Bobby Riggs on Sept. 20, 1973. With 30,472 people in attendance at the Houston Astrodome and 50 million television viewers looking on at home, King easily won the match that she said was less about tennis than about social change and gender equality.

Babe Ruth was not only the most fearsome hitter of his time, but also the most popular. A showman on and off the field, Ruth was equally comfortable as a commerical pitchman, a movie actor or the center of an adoring throng of fans.

Raising the techniques of rebounding to an elegant art form, Boston's crafty Bill Russell (6) dominated the NBA boards for 13 seasons, averaging 22.5 rebounds per game in the regular season and 24.9 in the playoffs.

Joe Willie Namath is not to be fully understood by most of us, of course. We are ancient, being over 23, and perhaps a bit arthritic, seeing as how we can't do the Duck. We aren't comfortably tuned in to the Mamas and the Uncles—or whatever their names are. We have cuffs on our trousers and, freakiest of all, we have pockets we can get our hands into. But Joe is not pleading to be understood. He is youth, success, the clothes, the car, the penthouse, the big town, the girls, the autographs and the games on Sundays. He simply is, man.

—Dan Jenkins
Oct. 17, 1966

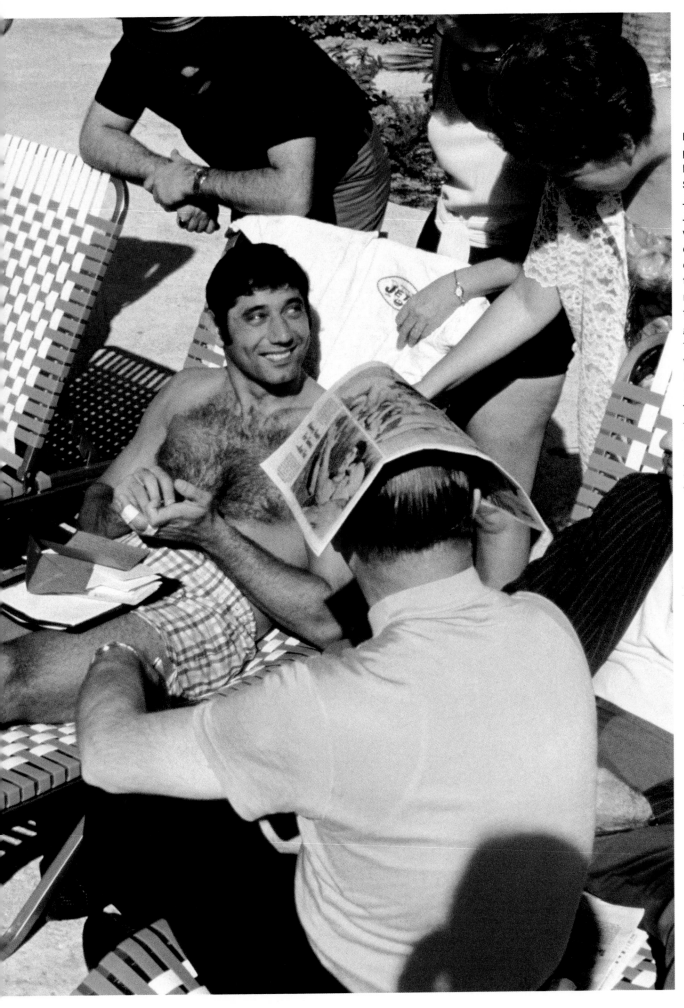

Holding court poolside in Miami Beach before Super Bowl III, Jets quarterback Joe Namath provided memorable copy for a bevy of sportswriters; the boldest pronouncement of the week was his guarantee that the AFL's Jets would defeat Baltimore of the NFL. When New York pulled off the improbable 16–7 victory, Namath's status as sports legend was assured.

The NBA All-Star
weekend in
1989 featured
fan-friendly
competition such
as the slam-dunk
contest, won
by Kenny Walker
of the New York
Knicks, whose
score was
aided by this
impressive feat
of levitation.

As the successor to Joe DiMaggio in center field for the Yankees, Mickey Mantle—he of the no-holds-barred swing—faced daunting expectations. In the end he lived up to them, claiming the 1956 Triple Crown, helping the Yankees win seven World Series and being named MVP of the league three times.

Satchel Paige, the brilliant Negro League fireballer who spent his most productive seasons with the Kansas City Monarchs, joined the Cleveland Indians as a 42-year-old major league rookie in 1948, one of countless black ballplayers whose season in the sun was greatly shortened by major league baseball's racist color bar.

Magic Johnson pulled another spectacular postseason performance out of his hat in 1988 to help the Lakers win their fifth title of the decade, averaging 21.1 points, 13 assists, 5.7 rebounds and two steals per game in the seven-game NBA Finals victory over the Detroit Pistons.

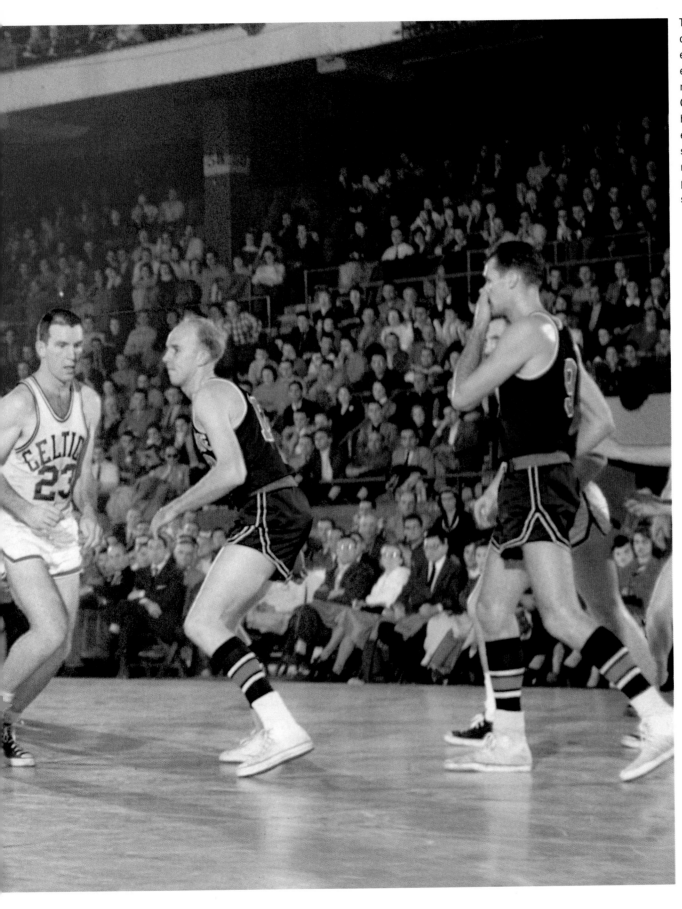

The Celtics'
dynasty was pow-
ered in its earli-
est years by the
masterful Bob
Cousy, in whose
hands dribbling
evolved from a
strictly defense
maneuver into a
powerful offen-
sive weapon.

Jackie Robinson's courage in breaking baseball's color line in 1947 with the Brooklyn Dodgers was mirrored on the field by his daring baserunning and aggressive hitting. By the time he retired in 1956, he had stolen home an incredible 19 times.

AFTERMATH

The end of Robinson's ten-year career coincided with the Dodgers' final year in Brooklyn. He was elected to the Baseball Hall of Fame in 1962, his first year on the ballot. Robinson remained a public figure as a commercial pitchman and a vice president at Chock Full o' Nuts. A political and civil rights activist, he urged blacks to "become producers, manufacturers ... and creators of businesses, providers of jobs." Never one to shy away from provocative views, Robinson publicly expressed his dissatisfaction with the NAACP, claiming that the group was not aggressive enough about civil rights, and he refused to attend old-timers' games in protest against baseball's lack of black managers and executives.

Weakened by heart disease and diabetes, Robinson died in 1972 at age 53. The Rev. Jesse Jackson delivered the eulogy at his funeral, noting Robinson's challenges and struggles on and off the field and concluding, "Jackie Robinson stole home and he's safe."

Arthur Ashe became the first African-American man to win the U.S. Open, when he triumphed at Forest Hills as an amateur in 1968. After retiring in 1980 with 33 career titles, he became a dignified advocate for minorities in the game, and captained the U.S. Davis Cup team from 1980 to '85.

The preeminent player of his, and possibly any, generation, Pete Sampras has won 11 Grand Slam titles—including four U.S. Opens and five Wimbledons—one shy of alltime leader Roy Emerson's total.

Photography Credits

Front Cover
Fernando Medina/NBA Photos.

Back Cover
Heinz Kluetmeier.

Front Matter
Half-title page, Corbis-Bettmann;
Title page, Neil Leifer.

Introduction
6, Corbis-Bettmann; 7, Sheedy & Long; 8–9, V.J. Lovero.

Memorable Moments
10–11, Andy Hayt; 12, Mike Powell/Allsport U.S.A.; 14–15, Walter Iooss Jr.; 16–17, Ralph Crane/Life; 18, Neil Leifer; 19, Ronald C. Modra; 20–21, Richard Mackson; 22–23, Walter Iooss Jr.; 24–25, Freelance Photographers Guild; 26, David Burnett/Contact Press Images.; 27, Neil Leifer; 28–29, John Iacono; 30–31, Marvin E. Newman; 32–33, Walter Iooss Jr.; 34, Heinz Kluetmeier; 35, Heinz Kluetmeier; 36–37, John Iacono; 38, Heinz Kluetmeier/ABC Sports; 39, Hy Peskin; 40–41, Walter Iooss Jr.; 42, Corbis-Bettmann; 43, Corbis-Bettmann.

Record Breakers
44–45, Corbis-Bettmann; 47, National Baseball Library and Archive, Cooperstown, New York; 48, Corbis-Bettmann; 48–49, Walter Iooss Jr.; 50, Corbis-Bettmann; 51, Heinz Kluetmeier; 52–53, John G. Zimmerman; 54, Walter Iooss Jr.; 55, *The Sporting News*; 56–57, Walter Iooss Jr.; 58–59, Heinz Kluetmeier; 60–61, John G. Zimmerman/Life; 62, Ronald C. Modra; 63, Culver Pictures; 64–65, Bill Eppridge/Life; 66, Walter Iooss Jr.; 67, Süddeutscher Verlag; 68–69, Neil Leifer; 70, Tony Duffy/Allsport; 71, Steve Goldstein; 72–73, Oxford Mail; 74, Co Rentmeester/Life; 75, Hy Peskin/FPG; 76, The Durant Collection; 77, John G. Zimmerman; 78–79, Jonathan Daniel; 79, Corbis-Bettmann.

Big Events
80–81, James Drake; 83, James Drake; 84-85, Manny Millan; 86, © *New York Daily News;* 87, Neil Leifer; 88–89, Walter Iooss Jr.; 90–91, Herb Scharfman/Life; 92–93, Neil Leifer; 94, Walter Iooss Jr.; 94–95, Manny Millan; 96–97, Al Tielemans; 98–99, George

Tiedemann; 100–101, Walter Iooss Jr.; 102–103, National Baseball Library and Archive, Cooperstown, New York; 104, Peter Read Miller; 105, Corbis-Bettmann News Photos; 106, James Drake; 107, John G. Zimmerman; 108–109, AP/Wide World Photos; 110, Rich Clarkson; 111, Peter Read Miller; 112–113, Hy Peskin; 114, John G. Zimmerman; 115, Damian Strohmeyer; 116–117, Walter Iooss Jr.; 118, Chuck Solomon; 119, Manny Millan; 120, Heinz Kluetmeier; 121, Neil Leifer.

Athletes
122–123, Walter Iooss Jr.; 125, James Drake; 126–127, National Baseball Library and Archive, Cooperstown, New York; 128–129, John W. McDonough; 130–131, Bill Frakes; 132–133, Herb Scharfman; 135, Grey Villet/Life; 136–137, Neil Leifer; 138–139, Sam Forencich; 140, James Drake; 141, Neil Leifer; 142–143, John Biever; 144, Heinz Kluetmeier; 145, Walter Iooss Jr.; 146–147, Stefan Warter; 148–149, Sam Forencich/NBA Photos; 150–151, Marvin E. Newman; 152–153, Corbis-Bettmann; 154, Walter Iooss Jr.; 155, © Jerry Cooke; 156–157, Associated Press; 158–159, Walter Iooss Jr.; 160–161, Walter Iooss Jr.; 162–163, Walter Iooss Jr.; 164–165, Associated Press; 166, Richard Mackson; 167, National Baseball Library and Archive, Cooperstown, New York; 168–169, Hy Peskin; 170–171, Corbis-Bettmann; 172, Manny Millan; 173, Claudio Edinger.

Index